All About
Elephants

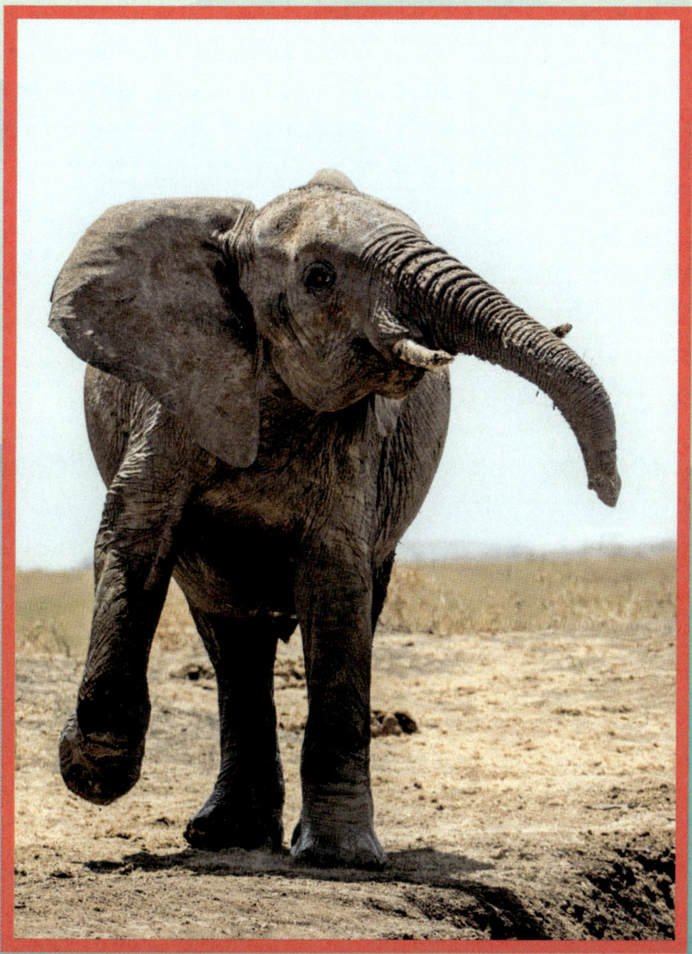

EDventure
LEARNING

How to Use This Book

This book is part of our Read Together series, a collection of books designed to be enjoyed by a young reader paired with a more experienced reader, such as a parent, grandparent, or older sibling. Take turns reading out loud together.

 The pages on the left side are meant for the younger reader. These pages use short, simple sentences and larger print. They are marked at the bottom of the page with the symbol shown at left.

The right-side pages are for the older reader. They contain paragraphs with longer sentences and more complex vocabulary. These pages are marked at the bottom of the page with the symbol shown at right.

Shared reading helps new readers gain confidence. It's also a great way for all ages to bond over books. We hope you enjoy this book as you Read Together.

Copyright © 2020 by EDventure Learning LLC

All rights reserved. This book or any portion thereof may not be reproduced or used in any manner whatsoever without the express written permission of the publisher.

Printed in the United States of America
Paperback ISBN: 978-1-64824-016-4

EDventure Learning LLC
5601 State Route 31 #1296
Clay, NY 13039

www.edventurelearning.com
Email us at hello@edventurelearning.com

Table of Contents

What Elephants Look Like .... p. 4

Where Elephants Live .... p. 14

What Elephants Do .... p. 18

Glossary .... p. 28

Index and Credits .... p. 29

What Elephants Look Like

Elephants are very big!

Elephants are the largest land animals in the world. There are two main types- African elephants and Asian elephants. African elephants are the larger of the two. An adult African elephant is 8-13 feet (2.4-4.0 m) tall and weighs 5,000-14,000 pounds (2,268-6,350 kg). Asian elephants are a little smaller, standing 6.5-12 feet (2.0-3.7 m) tall and weighing 4,500-11,000 pounds (2,041-4,990 kg).

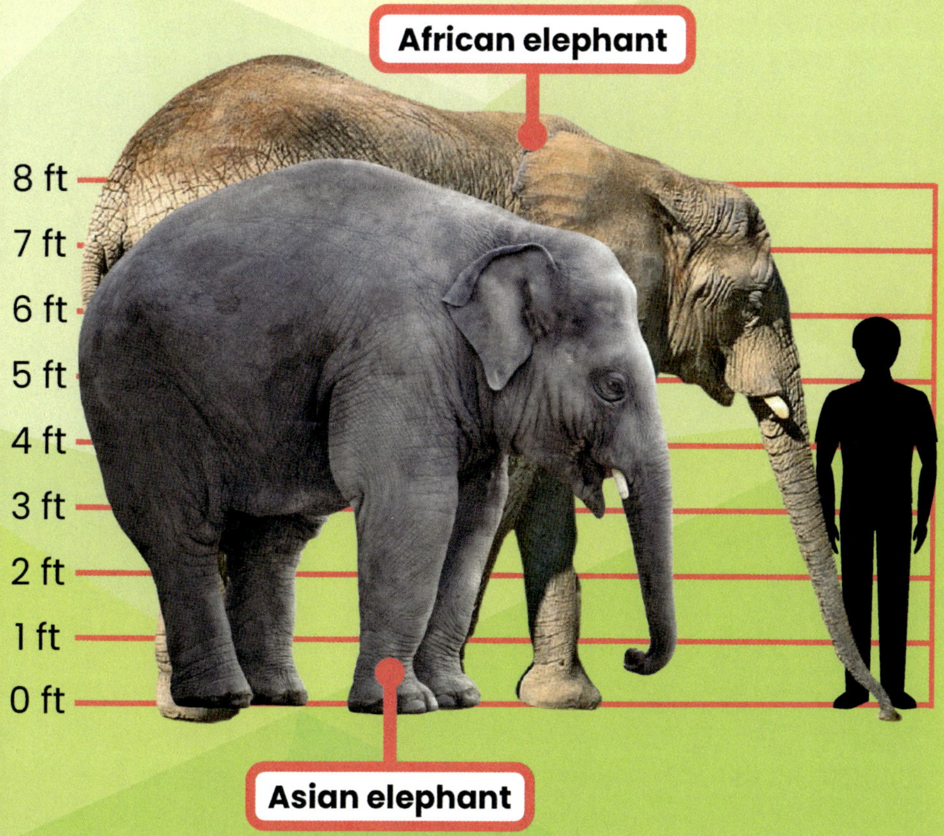

African elephant

8 ft
7 ft
6 ft
5 ft
4 ft
3 ft
2 ft
1 ft
0 ft

Asian elephant

They have gray or brown skin.

Elephants have thick, wrinkly skin that is either gray or brown. Sometimes even gray elephants look a little brown because they often cover themselves in dirt and mud to cool off.

Young Asian elephants have some brown hair, but they lose it as they get older.

They have trunks.

An elephant's trunk is a long body part that combines the nose and the upper lip. Like any other nose, a trunk is used to breathe and smell, but that's not all it can do! An elephant uses its trunk to eat, spray water, pick up objects, make sounds, and more. It can even use its trunk like a snorkel so that it can breathe underwater!

Many elephants have tusks.

Tusks are long, pointed teeth that stick out of elephants' mouths. Both male and female African elephants can have tusks, but only male Asian elephants can grow them (and not all do). Elephants use their tusks for digging, lifting, and protecting themselves.

African elephant

They have big ears.

All elephants have large ears that hang from the sides of their heads. In addition to hearing, elephants' ears help them keep cool and communicate with each other.

Asian elephant

An easy way to tell African and Asian elephants apart is to look at their ears. African elephants have much larger ears that stick straight out sideways. They also come up above the top of the elephant's head. Asian elephants have smaller, rounder ears that sit lower and lay back closer to the side of the head.

Where Elephants Live

Some elephants live in Africa.

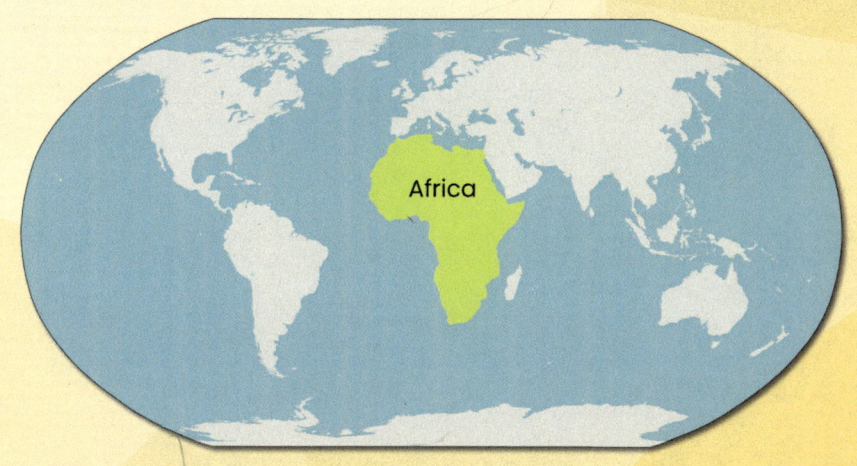

Most African elephants live in the **savanna**- flat plains covered in tall grass and scattered trees. Some African elephants live in forests, mountains, or deserts.

savanna

Some elephants live in Asia.

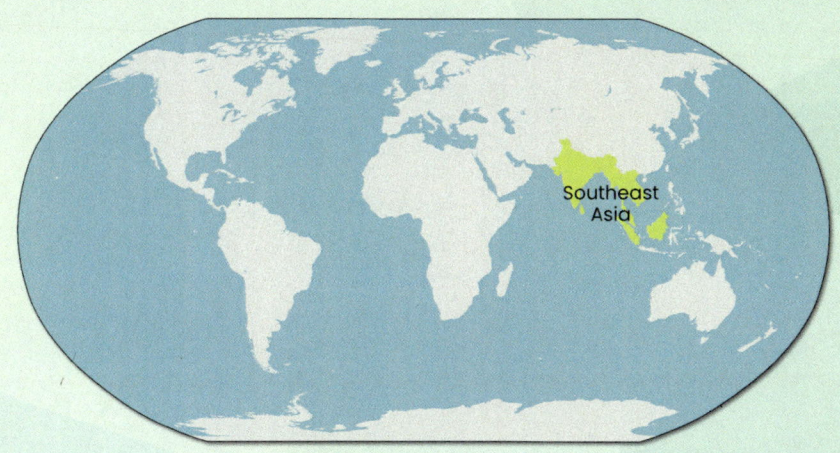

Asian elephants live in India and throughout Southeast Asia. These elephants live mostly in tropical forests.

What Elephants Do

They eat plants.

Elephants are **herbivores** who eat grasses, roots, leaves, fruit, and bark. It takes a lot of food to fill up such a large body. An elephant can eat as much as 300 pounds (136 kg) of food in one day.

They use their trunks to eat and drink.

Elephants use their trunks to grab their food and put it into their mouths. The end of an elephant's trunk has finger-like tips that help the animal grasp small objects. African elephants have two of these "fingers," while Asian elephants have one.

Elephants also use their trunks to help them drink. They suck up water into their trunks and then quickly spray the water into their mouths. They also spray water onto their bodies to cool off.

They walk far to find food.

Since elephants eat so much, they have to keep moving to find enough food. Elephants cover long distances in their search for more plants to eat.

They live in groups.

Elephants live in groups called **herds**. The herds are **matriarchal**, which means they are led by a female. The leader is usually the oldest and biggest female. Females and young elephants always stick together in herds. Adult males sometimes go off on their own or with a small group of other males.

They raise calves.

A baby elephant is called a **calf**. Elephants have one calf at a time. A calf learns to stand within minutes of birth and can walk after a few hours. African elephant calves can be born with short "baby tusks." These fall out after about a year, and permanent ones grow in their place.

Glossary

Calf
Baby elephant

Herbivore
Animal that eats only plants

Herd
Group of elephants

Matriarchal
Led by a female

Savanna
Plains with scattered trees and a warm climate

Index

A
African elephant, 5, 11-15, 21, 27

Appearance, 4-13, 27

Asian elephant, 5, 7, 11, 13, 16-17, 21

C
Calf, 7, 25-28

F
Food, 9, 18-23, 28

H
Habitat, 14-17

Herd, 24-25, 28

M
Movement, 23, 27

S
Savanna, 15, 28

T
Trunk, 8-9, 20-21

Tusk, 10-11, 27

Credits

The images in this book are used with permission as follows. Images not listed here are © EDventure Learning LLC.

Cover and title page: David Clode | Unsplash; Interior backgrounds: Kappy Kappy | Rawpixel; p. 3: Saifuddin Ratlamwala | Pexels; p. 4: Nam Anh | Unsplash; p. 5: Alexander Lesnitsky | Pixabay, Projekt Kaffeebart | Pixabay, Macrovector | Freepik; p. 6: Saad Khan | Unsplash; p. 7: Christoph Schutz | Pixabay (top), Dušan Smetana | Unsplash (bottom); p. 8: Usman Ashraf | Unsplash (top), Jevtic | Dreamstime (bottom); p. 9: Andrew Rice | Unsplash (top), Peter Betts | Dreamstime (bottom); p. 10: Amandad | Pixabay; p. 11: Rudy and Peter Skitterians | Pixabay; p. 12: Renato Conti | Pexels; p. 13: Jan Vašek | Pexels; p. 14: Jürgen Bierlein | Pixabay; p. 15: Clker Free Vector Images | Pixabay (top), Taylor Lee | Unsplash (bottom); p. 16: Lydia Casey | Unsplash; p. 17: Clker Free Vector Images | Pixabay (top), Saketh Upadhya | Unsplash (bottom); p. 18: Photos by Beks | Unsplash; p. 19: Jana V. M. | Pixabay; p. 20: Ana Frantz | Unsplash; p. 21: Jean Wimmerlin | Unsplash (top), Charl Durand | Unsplash (bottom); p. 22: Sergi Ferrete | Unsplash; p. 23: Matthew Spiteri | Unsplash; p. 24: Larry Li | Unsplash; p. 25: Rico Lotze | Pixabay p. 26: Katie Hollamby | Pexels; p. 27: Maud Cuenin | Pixabay (top), Lili Koslowksi | Unsplash (bottom); p. 28 (from top): Maud Cuenin | Pixabay, Ana Frantz | Unsplash, Larry Li | Unsplash, Maud Cuenin | Pixabay, Taylor Lee | Unsplash

Check out these other titles in the Read Together series!

All About Camels

All About Cheetahs

All About Giraffes

All About Elephants

All About Kangaroos

Keep in touch!

FOLLOW US ON SOCIAL MEDIA

   @edventurelearning

 www.edventurelearning.com

 Want freebies? Email us at **hello@edventurelearning.com** with the subject "Read Together" to join our newsletter and we'll send you free printables to keep the learning going!

All About Lions

All About Penguins

All About Polar Bears

All About Tigers

All About Zebras

Made in the USA
Las Vegas, NV
09 February 2024